Blue in Green

PHOENIX POETS

CHIYUMA ELLIOTT

Blue in Green

THE UNIVERSITY OF CHICAGO PRESS

Chicago and London

The University of Chicago Press, Chicago 60637
The University of Chicago Press, Ltd., London
© 2021 by The University of Chicago
Published 2021
Printed in the United States of America

30 29 28 27 26 25 24 23 22 21   1 2 3 4 5

ISBN-13: 978-0-226-78388-8 (paper)
ISBN-13: 978-0-226-78391-8 (e-book)
DOI: https://doi.org/10.7208/chicago/9780226783918.001.0001

Library of Congress Cataloging-in-Publication Data

Names: Elliott, Chiyuma, author.
Title: Blue in green / Chiyuma Elliott.
Other titles: Phoenix poets.
Description: Chicago : University of Chicago Press, 2021. | Series: Phoenix
   poets | Includes bibliographical references.
Identifiers: LCCN 2020047073 | ISBN 9780226783888 (paperback) | ISBN
   9780226783918 (ebook)
Subjects: LCGFT: Poetry.
Classification: LCC PS3605.L4452 B59 2021 | DDC 811/.6—DC23
LC record available at https://lccn.loc.gov/2020047073

for KATIE & EMMY LOU

Be constant in
inconstancy, love,
be the kingfisher
flying from the wire.

—W. S. Di Piero, "The Heart"

CONTENTS

ACKNOWLEDGMENTS

Grateful acknowledgment is due to the editors of the following publication where these poems first appeared:

Jazz and Culture: "J-572 (431) I" and "Composition No. 152"

"I imagined all the place-names as code" was first published in *America, We Call Your Name: Poems of Resistance and Resilience* (San Francisco: Sixteen Rivers Press, 2018).

A number of poems in this book, "*Landscape* is a word with fraught connotations," "Blue in Green," "If I Asked You To," "The Fox Emerging from Shadow," and "The Winter Mirror," are forthcoming in *The Black Geographic: Praxis, Resistance, Futurity*, edited by Camilla Hawthorne and Jovan Scott Lewis (Durham: Duke University Press, forthcoming).

So many thanks are due to the poets and teachers who buoy me up: Katie Peterson, Kimmy Grey, Rick Barot, Van Jordan, Rowan Ricardo Phillips, Ross White, Dana Koster, Andrew Saulters, and Karen Brennan. And to Audre Lorde, whose books were some of my earliest teachers about introspection, blackness, productive anger, and thematic range. I'm also grateful to my students at the University of California, Berkeley: fierce readers, and fiercely committed writers.

Blue in Green

WHEN I WAS A WAVE

I was willing to drink anything.
I found myself out gazing at stars.
The fishnets—
I played them like harps,

I said *promise me*,
and he left his clothes
on the shore, he waded in.
What I heard was polyphony.

I tried to persuade the moon,
but it stayed tethered.
When I swallowed, I remembered
how I hated all clocks,

that I wanted to quit.
I staked everything
on the churned-up sand
just beyond the tide line.

Let me tell you a story:
I loved. The days passed.
I sang the same old songs.
I left. I came back.

LAST WILL AND TESTAMENT

This twelvemonth,
the birds sat on the housetops;
the little minutes were four thousand books.
On the table, such odd trifles
kept your attention. Young lovers met;
some of what you heard
was the sea. Come away.
Let the grey paper confer
with the eggshells
and the brass horse.
Let summer wash its face
and stand in the pasture
and gather up its green buttons.
For pleasure is flowers on the table,
and you are *non plus*.
What I had, I spent on flowers.

NEVER MIND WHY

Never mind why, but once, my mother wrote to me
about the wild pigs. Their fascination
with the wood pile. The premise was time
and materials—pigs, earth, wood.
It wasn't a dream
because it didn't fold.

In the actual dream, there were large vases
filled with branches on all the tables.
Some were studded with orange fruits
that were not meant to be eaten
because of the tax status of the orchard.
It was puzzling, though my grandfather
would have negotiated a deal like that
for trees. And yet, the same old emotions
on being told to look but not to touch.
The napkins were dark damask,
which, in context, seemed crass.

Never mind why, but when my mother wrote to me
about the wild pigs, I thought about
chasing off the wild dogs. Brandishing a mattock
that morning, when the grass
was still wet around my ankles.
How they turned out not to be wild,
just loose and inquisitive. How it felt
to stand in the yard, observed by the burro,
and the grapevine, and the rabbits,
and, of course, the oaks.

I wanted to slap my husband
when he quoted Deuteronomy at breakfast.
Fires were burning other people's houses,
and the smoke kept wafting toward us.
It settled over the bay like a brown fog;
it turned the sun red. It wasn't a dream.
There was no good explanation.
First thing, I refilled the bird bath,
and again and again
over the course of the day,
like the water was a haven.

LANDSCAPE IS A WORD WITH FRAUGHT CONNOTATIONS

Of belonging, they say it's like a valley, and they say decolonize your desires, and *who says that*, you say. For example: when describing some small, unreasonable incident by a curb or a door.

I'm hemming this half-finished napkin because I thought I could make it rain; I thought the pervasive grey would amplify my feelings of contentment.

Without meaning to, I place a grid over everything and myself in the foreground, the world suddenly in thirds (like a sectioned orange fruit).

I thought I could make it rain all day; I thought the awkwardness engendered by the weather would amplify my feelings.

Largesse is a word I want to slot. They say it's like rock. And perhaps that means the perfect vantage: terraced land and trees full of heavy, unripe olives.

Outcroppings sometimes resemble a tumble of linen. I want to take advantage of the diffuse light—like climbers do.

WORKS ON PAPER

I.

Once we were fire. We pretended to be asleep,
eeling in the cloth over and over.
You were a municipal tower;
I was a picture book. When I felt flushed,
you said my hands
were quadratic equations;
when you felt flushed, I gave you shells
and arbitrary borders.

II.

I'm speaking
to the ghost data;
I'm speaking of blue ballast
& the swallows & the jonquils &
of course I think about
the early loss of love.
I'm speaking of migration,
that precocious moral territory
in the sand & the momentary bedlam
of a parallel ejected self.

III.

Atoms are so much easier, he said. And I was back there
suddenly, sitting at a small desk near the blackboard,
copying a diagram of the House of Atreus.
It was his windbreaker: a blue portal. It was the way
the ferns whispered, *Whither wander thou?*
Last weekend, I wandered. I admired the wisteria.
The sky was blue, so everyone was walking
and pointing out red berries and taking selfies,
maps in hand, vaguely aiming for the koi pond.
I was thinking about something wilder—
with moss, yes, but also ricochet and damp, and
last weekend, I insisted that someone learn
to throw an axe; last weekend, I kept asking
for directions. And the cherry trees were blooming.
And I was by a river. Last weekend, I was in Oregon.
And I was a child again, and it ached.

THE LION-WHEEL

I had the dream again. I was teaching; I couldn't find the roll book; I knew no one's name but my own. And the Lion-Wheel rolled in with its loud gold fur and tiny roar (teeth for spokes). The children were delighted, and they refused to pay attention. Did I mention I was in the future? A jay was jumping on the metal porch roof, and it woke me.

THE FOX EMERGING FROM SHADOW

The fox emerging from shadow is not the fox
    I meant to find a casket of seed beads
the empty drawer is the color of foxes
    it reminds me of strawberries
thank you says the note for your concern
    and how are you (how are you) it says
how long the nights are how interminable
    the fox is not the color of my sweater
the days are long and probably insincere
    you ate them so greedily I remember
the strawberries how resolutely you said it:
    the fox is not emerging
    the night is not cold, nor is it red
but that's not the reason in thin slanting cursive
    and that's not the fox nor is it the shadow

THE WINTER MIRROR

(EXPLANATION)

One day, we watch the laundry: a neon frock
sings itself an aria in the flood. Restlessness
is the last ordinary map. You say *swim*
and mean a well-lit room (not the riptide
of dark linens).
Or direction is gratuitous, and life
is a blank anthem, and the angels
are blue glass bottles, and *goodbye*
goodbye a thousand times,
and only the strange
is true, and the bottles
lift their phenomenal eyes.

(BECAUSE YOUR EVERY SKIN IS STAMPED ON EVERYTHING)

the glass window, the dervish meadow, the cloth as real as sky, the water erasing the story because fictions are stamped on everything, and the water is constantly changing, and it emerges from that place.

(IN WINDOWS ACTING JUST LIKE LEAVES)

The miraculous grey zenith
The miraculous green creek
The flowers on the sleeve
The general sense of rain

(MAY NO ONE MAKE HOUSEHOLD GODS OF SONG)

Things are simply things. The wet cloth
is nearly transparent, and it speaks of letting go.
Things are simply contained. Or maybe heaven
is an island, or simply a hand, or the shadow of a hand
to fill your eye (not this plainness).

(THE OPEN LETTER OF THE LAW)

Where the fold begins,
a mirror is crafted,
said the father of the harp.

(LATER, ONE SUCCUMBS TO THE FILTHY YELLOW CURTAINS)

But I prefer the cistern,
with its antique genius.
I prefer that landscape—
the grass thick with rain,
a branch collapsed
by too much peach.

I GUESS IT MUST BE THE FLAG OF MY DISPOSITION

I was early; the air smelled of lit cigarettes,
and the man felt inevitable,
awkwardly pouring his bleachy liquid
along the stone base moldings.
The flags snapped.

When I was a wave, I guess I was also a train.
I thought, *What shall I offer in lieu?*
I guess I was also a bird
carrying a man on my shoulders,
unable to put him down.
You know how it goes:
a series of metallic gasps.

The grass grows and dies. Time passes
(just now 9:42 to 9:43). I was lucent.
I guess I was also a lunar storm, though never
the paths bordered with rosemary,
and never a series of scratch marks
on a doorframe, sprouting to mark
our vegetable nature. It was agony.
Sometimes he was so heavy,

his cuneiform buttons pressed into my neck,
and my craters filled with water.
Now it seems to me an object lesson
about the shifting distance between landmarks.

Or it means someone is weaving hopeful green stuff
from the litter on sidewalks,
stuff that bears its maker's name
in its warp or its weft.

IF I ASKED YOU TO

Sing me a song about impostors, buttons
Used in place of lost game pieces, scraps
Of newsprint someone kept for,
Saved for, no discernible reason, what
Thin paper does to the body in

Question: as it's rinsed, as someone
Who's ceded the spray leans back,
Hip against the tiles, the green band
At plate-rail height like a necklace—
Of emeralds? Like a ring

Of trees? And just outside it, the eyes
Of so many foxes—small bright disks
Reflecting. Theoretically,
Trees fell and were chipped,
A single grand gesture, like a ballet,

And the birds heard it all
And saw it all, the space between
Trees like tall windows, and the sweep
Of a hand, and the water
Cascading in x direction.

BLUE IN GREEN

Stop working against the world, I counseled myself. *Love the one you're with.*
Love the color green.
—Maggie Nelson, *Bluets*

I imagined mornings: two plates, a worn table.
Nights a composite of the same small things.

I chronicled the history of segregated boardwalks.
I stirred my coffee with improbable plastic straws.

I imagined falling on a slick surface. No,
you held fast. Or maybe you stood on tiptoe

and blew smoke out the high bedroom window.
Maybe we were arguing about paintings.

Maybe I just imagined the digressions. Your letter read
Dear Day in Mid-to-Late October,

of course I concluded there was never any ballast.
The clocks fell back.

The euphorbia argued their case in simple terms.
What happened? I watched the sky; I stood on tiptoe.

I downplayed the mystery; I carried it
in a compartment of my purse.

TINDER

There is only forgiveness and
its absence, a whetstone. Awkward slide
into image. There are only trees
and the absent sounds they make.
For instance, the eucalyptus.
I had not walked for days,
and it fell across the ravine.
Then the smoke cleared;
now I can reach up and touch it
like I cannot touch even people
I know quite well. And the places
an intrepid bird drilled holes
before doing other things—
even those.

The acid green inside
a newly separated acorn cap.
A hymn to evenness:
the mulch in two large piles
by the staid buildings.
If forgiveness were botanical,
my hands would find odd bits of metal
tossed along the path. And the wind,
in its weird way, quite innocent.

A BLESSING COMPARED TO A WINDOW

I die by the fistful. I look through the glass.
I die by the acre, one unit of measure.
Say the ridges are in the ground
instead of the window.
Say the day girds itself against the heat,
and the birds sing moderately,
their feet tiny arias
on the edge of a stone basin.
Did I mention dying? How the morning
blinks its bright eyes
as if astounded by my pluck?
My sad, thirsty agapanthus
measures its days in oxblood loafers
and the constraints of old buildings,
and it makes me flowers.

J-572 (431) 1

In the original, we were reputed
to feed on sand.
The sky was our street;

we were called a tassel.
We were the emblems of border guards
and coopers. You beheld time in me—

we were manipulated like cattle we huddled together
for warmth the sky had lights
and cloverleaf interchanges

we were manipulated with rosewater
we genuflected in winter
the sky had lanes

and headstones,
pine trees and chimes.

COMPOSITION NO. 311

I am *the* bluest
blue, I am *the* coat,
I am *the* shoe.
Do you often
know what to do?
Maybe *this* is a test
for you.

WATER, WATER, WATER

Maybe *this* is a nest
for you when I say
melody = true
and each one's
a song.

COMPOSITION NO. 152

Maybe the song is a fluke,
or maybe it means a dramatic view,
or it drinks from the lake and tells something
truetrue
during certain harvest festivals the pattern can be found inside
geodes and tendons
during certain harvest festivals the pattern can be found inside
June sun and April wind—

or maybe it means I will be
as the sky is blue
to you

A MUSICAL SENSE OF LIFE

Little cloud. Little etch:
for you a continent
a watch three houses
for you a hue. Then
I didn't know

WHEN I WAS A WAVE

The narcissus bloomed early, as if by consensus.
One lush winter, and they were all in hysterics.

The birds repeated, *hey sailor hey sailor.*
The nights were separated into *before* and *after.*

As if I wanted that riot. I turned pages
and noticed (in this order): bowl, apple, storm.

And then there was a lithe, uncomplicated hour.
(Love willed it so.)

And the nights were separated into *before* and *after.*

LET ME BE JUST A LITTLE BIT BITTER SO I REMEMBER:

The point is some of it was easy. Making lists. Paying to sit in a church pew on a weeknight, listening to acoustic guitar, then ambling home to dream of Segovia.

I went to work in a store. I woke up early to prove myself and thought too much about what to wear. I thought too much about water.

This made the world stranger. I acquired housewares. What I remember most vividly: the sense that we were dispersing. I did a few things I regret.

If I hadn't walked back to your car; if it hadn't reminded me of half-dead trees. If there'd been any wind. Or if, in the medians, there'd been flowers.

The point is some of it was easy. I woke up to acoustic guitar; I spent long weekends thinking.

The conventions require definitions for words like *fondness*. While waiting for a call once, I held up some envelopes, each one painted with a school of tiny fish.

DEAR LITTLE SONG,

What if I hadn't caught them?
Trout glistening in water.
What if the first two notes were propositions?
Two white rabbits, heads lifted from the grass.

I've missed the grass.
I've missed the wet pitch of the water's mirrors.
Only their mouths and ears were moving.
Say we're owed specific things.

I've missed the steep pitch of the water's ceilings.
I've missed the corner of the bed, reflected in water.
And your little house (somewhere), its high cupboards
full of folded newspapers, crocheted blankets.

As glitter is to lake.
Like sunlight is to ache, like ache is to mountains.

A STORY ABOUT LONGING

I've fastened my voice with a stitch
I've stitched so neatly
it doesn't show.

I've delighted the stitch
with my tongue.
I still have a thicket of questions.

If the last thing you said wasn't garbled.
If you'd walked into the woods without speaking.
I've thicketed my tongue

with yellow thread.
If you paused first,
as if about to pour.

If you walked into the woods.
A brook runs through it.
Little wince of light,

little thicket of questions.
If your heart were wax.
If your heart were my tongue.

If a brook runs through it,
I've fastened some of its fish
with silver wire.

DEAR PAST AND FUTURE METASTASIS,

The women sitting next to me in the bakery
are talking about mammograms.
In one story, the radiologist is young
and thus recommends a second test.
In another, the doctor says,
re clinical trials, *participation is free,
and no harm will come to you.*

Someone says, *How are you?*
and I say, *Vertical*. Because lying is wrong,
and the whole truth is tactless.
The time I said, *gill net*, I meant, *look here*.
And *biopsy* meant *two hypotheses about rain*.

Remember when you called me artless?
It wasn't a coincidence.
I was trying to describe
that faded Vermeer print:
at first it looked like
any seaside shop front, but the point
was that it wasn't.

Re fables: to go where you go, and do
what you do, and then be buried there
is a raw deal. Re rawness: a colposcopy
begins with vinegar (a natural indicator).
Or rather, it begins with a video tutorial
about the body in relation to a speculum.

Began, I should say. Used in a sentence:
The tutorial *began*, and I concluded
I had little patience. The husband
of one of the women in the bakery
began by inventing a mammography machine,
the premise of which was cupping
(not squishing) the breasts.
Then he incorporated.

I keep thinking about yoga,
its cache of promises, like
what's possible on your mat
is possible in your life.
Alas, you are like that.

MY THROAT IN THE FIELD

For as long as I've known, I've been afraid. I've collected blue and green bottles to catch the light. I've threaded buttons on string. At night, I sewed the patches on with grey-green thread

and wandered through fields, the sound of waves in my ears, my throat a knot. Then I stood very still and asked to know everything. Nothing changed, despite the voice in my head.

Though it's only halfway into Monday, I've already made several mistakes, and I've barely left the house. I wonder how you explain it, when you get sick. To those who would expect a thorough accounting . . .

Any rents in the firmament? they ask.

I IMAGINED ALL THE PLACE-NAMES AS CODE

As a way of approaching a river; a kind of gill net.
Willamette and Chehalis; verso and recto.

As aperture. As moon in Libra. Absolute somehow.
As one who says simply, *you ask me and thus.*

I think I imagined a kind of beak. I think I imagined
a list of longish words. As one might philosophize

about the thaw while pumping gas;
the way one might pump gas, staring blankly

at the small red blizzard of numbers,
seeing a school of fish.

I have always imagined paradise
as doing many things in a small space.

Oh, tarp. Oh, evergreens in snow—
there is no one to tell this story to.

OBJECT STATE TIME SPACE CERTAINTY

The thing I learned was leopard spotted, it was pigment on plaster. The thing I learned was worth more than rubies (or so I was told). I was told I was cypress, elegant and cobwebbed, ever steady. I explained the state I was in with elaborate maps and colorful legends.

I learned brevity. I learned *of* brevity. Before there was breath on the water, or fish in it, there was nothing but brevity. I learned to wait. I acted quiet.

The thing I learned was ransacked. It was plucked from my setting (or so I was told). I drew breath. I was thoughtful, in the way fish elaborate water. I explained it with my feet. And I acted all the parts, condensing characters for the sake of brevity.

THE PLAY WITHIN

While it lasted, I meant to compose a letter. I meant to grow like Topsy and thought I'd resemble the citrus trees that reach over the fence tops along Airport Boulevard.

While it lasted, the silk waves billowed in the spotlights. The figures chanted, holding their corners tight like bedsheets. But the nosegays fooled no one, and there were parakeets in the lobby. Even I was ready for something.

I was ready for something like October. But the dream always ended by Lake Merritt, with unreasonable demands about charcoal grills, some geese looking on, and those match-height strangers standing by a diminutive mast.

THE FIRE THAT CONSUMES ALL BEFORE IT

for Jimmy B

fire altar • fire amel • fire and fury • fire and (the) sword (also fire and iron) •
fire-barrow • fire beacon • fire-bearing • firebed •
—*Oxford English Dictionary*

Like blades cutting a field, I marshaled
my forces, I forced my breath.

While I was waiting on the lawn,
the fawn-like candor
of the reindeer sculptures

(improbable citizens
made of bulbs and white wire)

seemed to say, *fight fire*
with fire; light fire with fire.

DEAR ILIUM,

Some of those battles were pointless.
I opened the tent flaps and peered out at the world.

The bird learned to copy so many sounds;
its entrails were clogged with bright bits of plastic.

What was our strategy again?
And why did the wind wince

as it skirted the brilliant corners downtown?
Some of those battles were jointless,

footless, feckless. Yet I polished the armor
and sat on the ground

and shot no sheriffs and smoked no spliffs
and sang songs that applied no pressure

when we ran out of bandages.
But some of those battles were spotless.

The signs said *fuck 12*, the seconds ticked past.
The thoughtless old ships rusted in the bay.

We lost we won we painted
new ships and faces on plywood,

and the birds wheeled and sang.
What's a victory, what's a garden?

We burned some cities,
we shattered some glass.

A LETTER

Care for winter
is a furious brown paper
which prompts us,

and sleep is sudden
within us and the earth.

A PROGRAM FOR CONTROL OF *OF*

At the risk of projecting
fierce love onto the landscape,
the story begins with spring
and proceeds by keening.
Or it begins with
the two of them
laughing warily.

If she sat on the shore
and foretold, and he listened,
then he became the shore.
It was one way
of minimizing risk.

If he gazed steadily
into the grate
and let his mind wander,
then he became ether.

If this forbids our opening
with the sunset's clipped
and many colors,
it also enjoins us
to weave flowers into our hair.

And if this, too, reminds us
of the earth thawing,
it also chastens:
their expressions are unreadable,
the spoons insist
against the sides
of so many half-full glasses.

DEAR TRANSFORMATION,

You owe me four legs and innumerable eyes.
I am writing to settle up.
In the place where empathy should be,
I found instead a slick black rock.
I learned to chip at it, to fashion
small sharp things inside.
They are working their way to the surface,
albeit slowly. You owe me a shelf of canisters
and a long skein of yarn.
In the place where empathy should be,
I found a tesseract. I was not familiar
with tesseracts, so I called it Sam
and made it the center
of a detailed cosmology.
I read it bedtime stories
that featured peaches and lamps
and displaced creatures.
Ambition was a balm, and all the balloons
floated successfully over vast green seas.
You owe me more than a thousand nights.
Instead of empathy, I found a set of keys.
The landscape lacked striation,
which now seems apposite.
Do you recognize the language?
I made it when you were sleeping,
and the city tilted beyond
the high panes of windows,
glowing pegs
in a black perforated screen.

Beauty falls from the hair.
You owe me sheaves of wheat
and also their safe storage.
You owe me the changing courses
of at least seven rivers
and enough potash
to shift the firing temperature
and a cavernous silence.
Yet these coins seem real enough.
There are flags around the perimeter.
I will never get all the sand
out of my pockets.

A WARNING

There are plenty of cautionary tales,
so here's another: if the sea was a coat,
then I was its sleeve. If the sea was a sleeve,
I was its loose button.
There are plenty of warnings
about seeing yourself in water.
I was also the bird and the smelt in its mouth.
If I'm crazy for feeling so,
what about how the rain seeps in
to the coat you almost didn't bring
because of all that sunlight?
Maybe I began by making paper boats.
If I let go of the boats, then they bobbed
as if nodding to different songs.

FOR GHOSTED GIRLS

We need a new name for the doubt
(they say *azure* here,
but blue will do). We need a new name
for north, a name for south,
a name for this place
where the tide rolls out.

A name for tales of tall black pots,
for button willows
and forget-me-nots.
We need a new name for lips,
a new name for eyes, a name
for waking up slowly

to the disguise the fog makes.
For hills and streets and damp,
a new name for lists,
and listing, and listless,
and why, and why me,
and why us.

NOTES

"Last Will and Testament" is a mostly found poem based on Thomas Nashe's *Summer's Last Will and Testament*, except for the verb tenses.

The second stanza of "Works on Paper" remixes Will Alexander's *Compression & Purity* (San Francisco: City Lights Publishers, 2011).

"The Fox Emerging from Shadow" was inspired by Beth Cavener's sculpture *Through an Empty Place (The Fox Emerging from Shadow)*: http://sixthfinch.com/cavener.html.

Each section of "The Winter Mirror" remixes words from a poem (or poems) by Paul Hoover: "The Explanation," "The Reason," "American Ruins," "Winter (Mirror)," "Theory of Margins," "Blanco y Negro," and "Structuring Duration."

The title and the hopeful green stuff in "I guess it must be the flag of my disposition" come from Walt Whitman's "Song of Myself": the object lesson contained in his passage that begins, "A child said *What is the grass?* fetching it to me with full hands. . . ."

"Blue in Green" is an ekphrastic poem about Miles Davis's song of the same name (which may have been written, at least in part, by Bill Evans).

"A Blessing Compared to a Window" was inspired by Thomas Merton's "The Blessed Virgin Mary Compared to a Window" (especially the line "I die by brightness and the Holy Spirit").

"J-572 (431) I," "Composition No. 311," "Water, Water, Water," "Composition No. 152," and "A Musical Sense of Life" are part of a series of ekphrastic poems based on Anthony Braxton's compositions, many recorded in collaboration with Andrew Cyrille and Peter Niklas Wilson.

The title of the poem "Let me be just a little bit bitter so I remember:" comes from Justin Phillip Reed's "Carolina Prayer."

"A Story About Longing" riffs on William Everson's little wince of delight in the thicket from *Tendril in the Mesh* (reprinted in 1999 in *The Integral Years: Poems, 1966–1974* by Black Sparrow Press).

"I imagined all the place-names as code" is based on a photograph by Young Suh called *For Sale, 2012* (from the 2016 exhibit *Can We Live Here? Stories from a Difficult World*).

"object state time space certainty" (a poem about the act, the state, and the thing I learned) is indebted to Kenneth Burke's "Container and Thing Contained" in *A Grammar of Motives* (Berkeley: University of California Press, 1969).

"The Fire That Consumes All Before It" is for the oracle James Baldwin. Its title comes from Cy Twombly's *Ilium* series.

"A Letter" is a found poem made from a semantically nonsensical sentence by Noam Chomsky and a 1985 contest entry by C. M. Street, which attempted (in not more than one hundred words) to make Chomsky's sentence meaningful.

"A Program for Control of *Of*" quotes and remixes J. V. Cunningham's essay "Logic and Lyric: Marvell, Dunbar, and Nashe," particularly his translations of Horace, in *Tradition and Poetic Structure: Essays in Literary History and Criticism* (Denver: Alan Swallow, 1960).

"Dear Transformation," was also inspired by J. V. Cunningham's essay "Logic and Lyric: Marvell, Dunbar, and Nashe." The line "Beauty falls from the hair" is from Thomas Nashe's "A Litany in Time of Plague" (more often quoted as "beauty falls from the air" because of an early misprint in the text).

"A Warning" riffs on Shakespeare's *Love's Labour's Lost* and the artwork of Jean-Antoine Watteau, upon whose pastorals some stage sets for a late adaptation of the play were based.